Reflections for My Baby

AN ILLUSTRATED KEEPSAKE JOURNAL TO
RECORD MEDITATIONS AND MILESTONES
DURING YOUR BABY'S FIRST YEAR OF LIFE

This journal was given with gratitude to my child

_____

born

_____

by your loving mother

_____

Reflections for My Baby

AN ILLUSTRATED KEEPSAKE JOURNAL TO
RECORD MEDITATIONS AND MILESTONES
DURING YOUR BABY'S FIRST YEAR OF LIFE

Laura Buller

≡Bluestreak

an imprint of Weldon Owen International
PO Box 3088 San Rafael, CA 94912
www.weldonowen.com

© 2021 Weldon Owen

Library of Congress Cataloging in Publication data is available.

Printed in China

ISBN-13: 978-1-68188-704-3

10 9 8 7 6 5 4 3 2 1

Contents

INTRODUCTION

Becoming a parent is an unforgettable experience. The excitement at finding out the news. The sleepless nights when it all became real. The wonder of the first ultrasound scan. The pleasures and pitfalls of pregnancy. The indescribable joy of birth, and of seeing your tiny face. And . . . back to the sleepless nights. But as much as I want to remember everything, it's hard to take it all in. So I'm collecting all my thoughts in this journal. I want to remember it all—from your first gummy smile to the way I felt when watching you sleep. Then, I want to share it with you. The story of your early life is all your own. Little reminders on these pages prompt my memories, and there is a secret place at the back of the book to make a time capsule for you. As the song says, you are my sunshine, and this is for you.

A LETTER TO MY CHILD, FROM MY HEART TO YOURS

Written on

As I write this, I am in

CHAPTER ONE

Coming Soon

GETTING READY FOR A NEW ARRIVAL

EXPECTING

Life is always a rich and steady time
when you are waiting for something
to happen or to hatch.

– E. B. WHITE

This is when and where I found out I was expecting you

My emotions were

My partner felt _____

_____

_____

_____

_____

_____

_____

I shared the news with everyone by _____

_____

_____

_____

_____

_____

I couldn't wait to meet you because _____

_____

_____

_____

_____

A NEW LEAF ON THE FAMILY TREE

A baby is God's opinion that life should go on.

– CARL SANDBURG

My family reacted to the news about you by

Other children in the family said

I celebrated with the family by

_____

_____

_____

_____

_____

A family member I bonded with at that time was

_____

_____

_____

_____

One of the sweetest or funniest things a family member said about the news was

_____

_____

_____

_____

_____

PREPARING FOR A LITTLE ONE

A mother's joy begins when new life is stirring inside . . .
when a tiny heartbeat is heard for the very first time.

– UNKNOWN

Some of the things I did to get ready were _____

_____

_____

_____

_____

The first thing I bought was _____

_____

_____

_____

_____

_____

My circle of friends helped me by _____

_____

_____

_____

_____

_____

_____

_____

_____

My friends gave me this advice _____

_____

_____

_____

_____

_____

_____

_____

_____

_____

_____

_____

_____

US TOGETHER

Pregnancy is getting company inside one's skin.

– MAGGIE SCARF

My pregnancy felt

The best part was

The hardest part was

I didn't expect _____

_____

_____

_____

_____

When I first felt you move or kick it was _____

_____

_____

_____

_____

_____

We went everywhere together—including _____

_____

_____

_____

_____

_____

These are the sounds and voices you heard _____

_____

_____

_____

_____

_____

LITTLE WISHES

Babies . . . are like little bundles of hope.
Like the future in a basket.

– LISH MCBRIDE

These are the features or traits I hoped to pass down to you

And my dreams for what kind of parent I would become

I was ready for my life to change because _____

_____

_____

_____

_____

_____

What motherhood meant to me _____

_____

_____

_____

_____

_____

_____

As your due date got closer, I felt _____

_____

_____

_____

_____

_____

CHAPTER TWO

Welcome to the World

YOUR FIRST DAYS

HAPPY BIRTHDAY

Childbirth is more admirable than conquest, more amazing than self-defense, and as courageous as either one.

– GLORIA STEINEM

You were born on _____

_____

At (time) _____

_____

In _____

_____

And I named you _____

_____

I knew you were ready for the world when _____

_____

_____

_____

_____

These were the plans I had for your birth _____

_____

_____

_____

My feelings on the big day (or night!) were _____

_____

_____

_____

_____

My partner was feeling _____

_____

_____

_____

_____

Something funny that I remember was _____

_____

_____

_____

One thing I didn't expect was _____

_____

_____

_____

Here is the story of how we met for the very first time

YOUR FIRST DAY

*There are places in the heart you don't
even know exist until you love a child.*

– ANNE LAMOTT

I finally got to see you. You looked _____

_____

_____

_____

_____

I was surprised by _____

_____

_____

_____

_____

_____

_____

I dressed you in _____

_____

_____

_____

_____

_____

When I looked at you or held you, I felt _____

_____

_____

_____

_____

_____

_____

_____

My partner felt _____

_____

_____

_____

_____

_____

This is how you spent your first hours

_____

_____

_____

_____

_____

Something about you I found amazing right away was _____

_____

_____

_____

_____

_____

I was grateful for _____

_____

_____

_____

_____

When I was feeding you, I thought

_____

_____

_____

_____

_____

_____

The story of your first night

_____

_____

_____

_____

_____

_____

_____

_____

_____

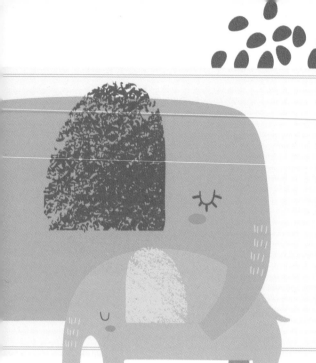

A FAMILY WELCOME

A baby is born with a need to be loved—and never outgrows it.

– FRANK A. CLARK

Your first family visitor (or visitors) was _____

_____

_____

_____

_____

Other family members and friends who stopped by were _____

_____

_____

_____

_____

_____

Here are some of the things they said _____

_____

_____

_____

_____

_____

_____

Some of the gifts they brought were _____

_____

_____

_____

_____

I was particularly happy when _____

_____

_____

_____

_____

_____

SWEET STORIES

The littlest feet make the biggest footprints in our hearts.

– UNKNOWN

Here are some memories about your first few days _____

_____

_____

_____

_____

_____

_____

_____

_____

_____

_____

_____

COMING HOME

Loving a baby is a circular business, kind of a feedback loop. The more you give the more you get and the more you get the more you feel like giving.

– PENELOPE LEACH

I brought you home on _____

_____

I'd describe the first days as _____

_____

_____

_____

_____

_____

_____

I felt happiest when _____

_____

_____

_____

Some of the tough parts were _____

_____

_____

_____

People who helped were _____

_____

_____

_____

It was all worth it when _____

_____

_____

_____

_____

CHAPTER THREE

Family Times

HOME TOGETHER

A HAPPY HOUSE

*A baby makes love stronger, the days shorter, the
nights longer, savings smaller, and a home happier.*

– UNKNOWN

This is where we lived when you were a baby

Here's who lived in the house with you

_____

_____

_____

_____

We had a pet called _____

_____

_____

_____

You slept in _____

_____

_____

_____

That room was special because _____

_____

_____

_____

_____

_____

MOMMY AND ME

The life of a mother is the life of a child:
you are two blossoms on a single branch.

– KAREN MAEZEN MILLER

Here is a letter to you about my feelings and experiences during the first few weeks of being your mother

YOUR VIPs

I don't know why they say you have a baby.
The baby has you.

– GALLAGHER

Important adults in your babyhood were _____

_____

_____

_____

You adored _____

_____

_____

_____

_____

_____

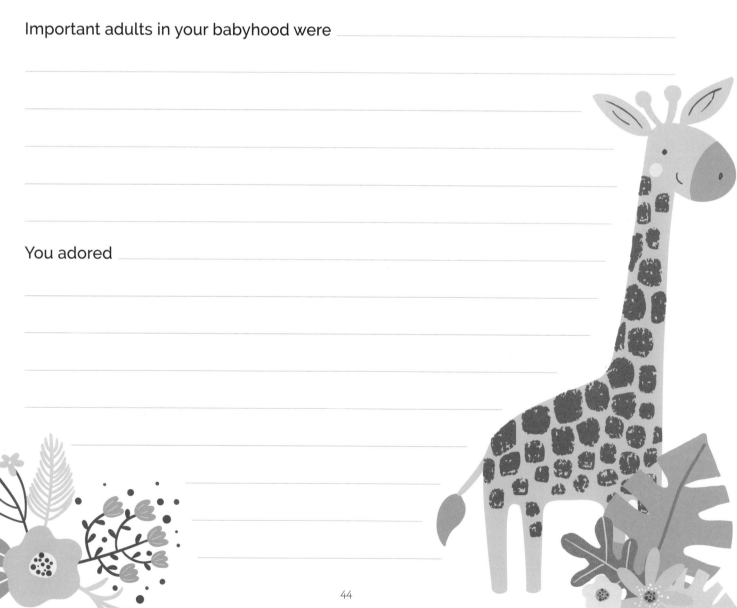

You were always comforted by a cuddle from

Someone who made you giggle was

Here's a memory of when you met your grandparent(s)

CELEBRATING WITH YOU

A new baby is like the beginning of all things . . .
wonder, hope, a dream of possibilities.

– EDA J. LESHAN

I celebrated your arrival by _____

_____

_____

_____

_____

_____

Some of the family traditions I hoped to carry on with you were _____

_____

_____

_____

_____

_____

And new traditions I wanted to start were

_____

_____

_____

_____

_____

_____

_____

This is how I ended each day with you _____

_____

_____

_____

_____

_____

_____

_____

Your first family celebration was _____

_____

_____

_____

_____

When you were together with my whole family, I felt _____

_____

_____

_____

_____

Something you did that made people smile _____

_____

_____

_____

_____

The first birthday party you went to was _____

_____

_____

_____

_____

The holiday we most enjoyed together was

Some of my best memories were

Some of your special holiday outfits were

CHAPTER FOUR

A Day in the Life

SETTLING IN TOGETHER

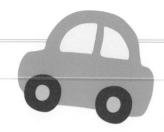

PLAYTIME

*Life is playfulness. We need to play so that
we can discover the magic all around us.*

– FLORA COLAO

One of the first objects I remember you reaching for was _____

_____

_____

_____

_____

Your favorite objects to explore were _____

_____

_____

_____

_____

Some of the toys you enjoyed as a baby were

The most chewed toy without a doubt was

Your favorite comfort object was

A toy handed down from another family member was

These are the ways you liked to play

_____

_____

_____

_____

_____

_____

_____

_____

You most enjoyed playing with _____

_____

_____

_____

_____

_____

_____

_____

_____

You were captivated by

You sometimes got frustrated when

Playing helped me get to know you because

OUT AND ABOUT

*There's nothing wrong with
having a tree as a friend.*

– BOB ROSS

One of the earliest times we went outside was _____

_____

_____

_____

_____

_____

We walked or hiked together by _____

_____

_____

_____

_____

These things in the big outdoors got your attention

_____

_____

_____

_____

_____

The first time you went to the playground was _____

_____

_____

_____

_____

_____

_____

You loved these outdoor activities _____

_____

_____

_____

_____

_____

A few stories about the different places we went and the things we did outside when you were a baby

_____

_____

_____

_____

_____

_____

_____

_____

_____

_____

_____

_____

_____

_____

_____

_____

_____

_____

MEALTIMES

You mean to tell me that spoons don't actually sound like airplanes?

– UNKNOWN

As a small baby, you mostly ate

You had feeding times

Your first solid foods were

The foods you liked to stick in your mouth yourself were

_____

_____

_____

_____

_____

Maybe the biggest food mess you ever made was _____

_____

_____

_____

_____

Your very favorite food was probably _____

_____

_____

I could tell because _____

_____

_____

_____

_____

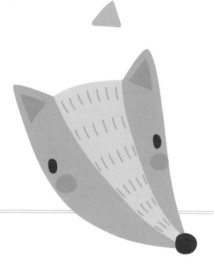

FUNNY FACES

*Every happy memory created for a child
is another treasure of a lifetime.*

– DONNA MARIE

Your favorite silly face was

A silly noise you really enjoyed was

A song we liked to share was

You didn't really like _____

_____

_____

_____

_____

This is how I felt when you smiled back at me _____

_____

_____

_____

_____

And your first giggles were _____

_____

_____

_____

_____

EXPRESSING YOURSELF

A person is a person no matter how small.

– DR. SEUSS

Before you could talk, you communicated with me by

_____

_____

_____

_____

You used to make different noises when you _____

_____

_____

_____

_____

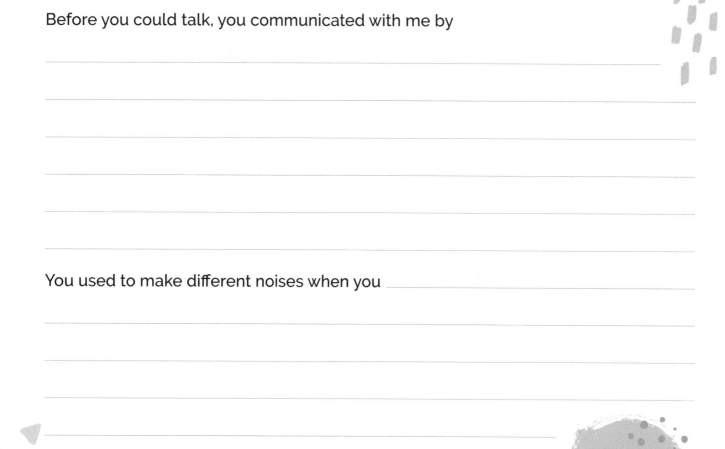

I could tell you were feeling happy when

You showed me you were hungry by

And I knew you were grumpy when

To cheer you up, I used to

STORYTIME

Books train your imagination to think big.

– TAYLOR SWIFT

Some of your favorite books were _____

_____

_____

_____

_____

_____

We read this book together a thousand times _____

_____

_____

_____

_____

A book you liked to read with someone else was _____

_____

_____

_____

_____

The character you loved the most was _____

_____

_____

_____

The pictures and photos in books that got your attention were _____

_____

_____

_____

_____

_____

MUSICAL
MOMENTS

*Music gives a soul to the universe, wings to the mind,
flight to the imagination, and life to everything.*

– PLATO

You loved to hear these songs over and over _____

_____

_____

_____

Our record for listening to the same song on repeat was _____

_____

_____

_____

Your favorite song with hand motions was _____

_____

_____

_____

The other kinds of music and songs you liked were

_____

_____

_____

_____

The first time you tried to sing along was _____

_____

_____

_____

_____

_____

A toy musical instrument you loved to play was _____

_____

_____

_____

_____

_____

_____

SLEEPYTIME

*People who say they sleep like a baby
usually don't have one.*

– UNKNOWN

When you were a baby, you slept like _____

_____

_____

Our bedtime routine was _____

_____

_____

_____

Bathtimes were _____

_____

_____

In the tub you liked to play with _____

_____

_____

The one toy you could never sleep without was

And your favorite pair of jammies was

Something that made it hard for you to sleep was

Something that helped you fall asleep was

A letter with love, to remind you of all the ways you made me happy when you were a baby

_____

_____

_____

_____

_____

_____

_____

_____

_____

_____

_____

_____

_____

_____

_____

CHAPTER FIVE

Exploring and Learning

GROWING UP

GETTING AROUND

His little hands stole my heart . . .
and his little feet ran away with it.

– UNKNOWN

This is how I felt when you started to crawl _____

_____

_____

_____

_____

Your favorite place to crawl was _____

_____

_____

_____

_____

_____

A few of your early mishaps

How you learned to walk

You used to make me laugh when

When you started dancing, you moved like

HELLO, YOU

Teaching is listening. Learning is talking.

– DEBORAH MEIER

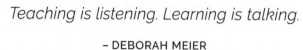

These are some of the sounds you made before you started talking

_____

_____

_____

_____

Your first word was _____

_____

_____

The next few words were _____

_____

_____

_____

_____

_____

Your favorite thing to say was _____

_____

_____

_____

_____

The funniest things you said were _____

_____

_____

_____

_____

You made up words like _____

_____

_____

_____

_____

This is how I felt when I first heard you say my name _____

_____

_____

_____

_____

HAVING FUN

Play is the work of children.

– MARIA MONTESSORI

Once you could walk, the activity you loved the most was _____

A game you liked to play with me was _____

Your favorite thing to do outside was _____

_____

_____

_____

_____

_____

When we went to the park, you made a beeline for the _____

_____

_____

_____

_____

_____

_____

When it was time to stop playing, you _____

_____

_____

_____

_____

PEOPLE IN YOUR WORLD

Love only grows by sharing.

– BRIAN TRACY

Your favorite people were

You loved going to see

You'd always give a hug or kiss to

Someone who babysat you was _____

_____

_____

_____

_____

A friend or sibling you played alongside was _____

_____

_____

_____

_____

_____

_____

If no one was around to play, you _____

_____

_____

_____

_____

_____

IMAGINE THAT

Every child is born blessed with a vivid imagination.

– WALT DISNEY

A few of the stories you made up for us _____

Your favorite things to draw were _____

_____

_____

_____

_____

Your favorite things to make were _____

_____

_____

_____

_____

_____

Sometimes it was more fun making a mess, like _____

_____

_____

_____

_____

You learned to use the computer or tablet when _____

_____

_____

_____

_____

YOUR FAVORITE THINGS

Children see magic because they look for it.

– CHRISTOPHER MOORE

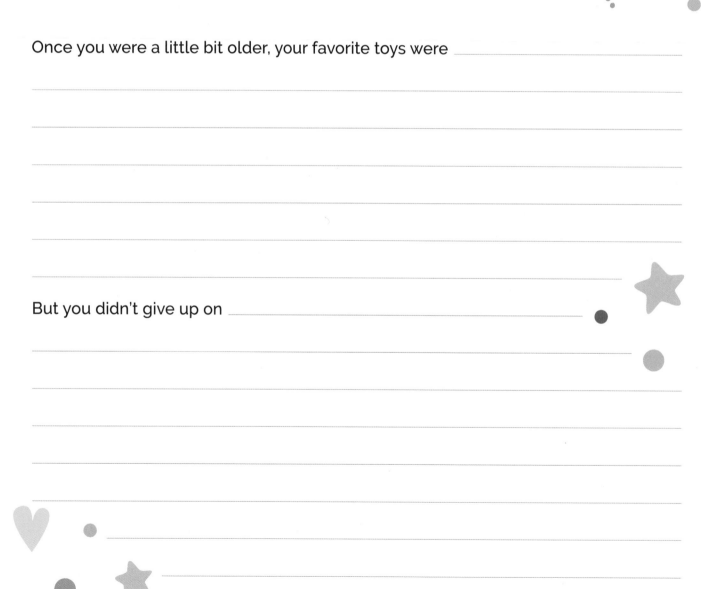

Once you were a little bit older, your favorite toys were _____

_____

_____

_____

_____

_____

But you didn't give up on _____

_____

_____

_____

_____

_____

_____

If we asked you to name the best thing in your room, it would be

_____

_____

_____

_____

If you could choose your own clothes every single day, you would wear _____

_____

_____

_____

_____

You liked to dress up as _____

_____

_____

_____

_____

The sweetest thing you ever made for me was _____

_____

_____

_____

_____

TREATS AND EATS

You can't buy happiness, but you can buy ice cream, and that is pretty much the same thing.

– UNKNOWN

You loved to eat _____

_____

_____

_____

But you weren't so keen on _____

_____

_____

_____

Something you learned to love was _____

_____

_____

_____

The best breakfast in the world to you was _____

_____

_____

_____

_____

Your ideal picnic would be _____

_____

_____

_____

_____

When we went shopping for food, you _____

_____

_____

_____

_____

The first time you helped out when we were cooking was

_____

_____

_____

_____

CHAPTER SIX

Hopes and Dreams

MY WISHES FOR YOUR FUTURE

LOOKING BACK

Don't look back unless you can smile;
don't look ahead unless you can dream.

– IRISH SAYING

My happiest memory from your early childhood was _____

_____

_____

_____

_____

_____

The hardest part of your early childhood was _____

_____

_____

_____

_____

_____

_____

I'll never forget when _____

_____

_____

_____

_____

_____

I'll always miss _____

_____

_____

_____

_____

_____

_____

_____

I was so proud of you when _____

_____

_____

_____

_____

_____

LOOKING FORWARD

Do not follow where the path may lead. Go instead where there is no path and leave a trail.

– RALPH WALDO EMERSON

I hope to see you grow to become _____

_____

_____

_____

_____

_____

_____

_____

_____

_____

_____

_____

I want you to remember

I know you'll be great at

I'll always be there to

MY MESSAGE TO YOU

My story in this book is finished, but yours is just beginning. Here is a message from me to you, with all my love and wisdom.

_____

_____

_____

_____

_____

_____

_____

_____

_____

_____

_____